PROPHETIC POETIC EXPRESSIONS

VOLUME 1

YVONNE PETERSON

ISBN-10:061591912X
ISBN-13: 978-0615919126(Focused Faith Publishing)

Prophetic Poetic Expressions

Printed in the United States of America

Dedication

Lord, I thank you for bringing me to "A Moment like this."

Theo! Teddy! All I can say is, "Ain't no stopping us now, we're on the move!"

Acknowledgements

Dr. Estela Beckford, thank you for gifting me with this awesome, anointed book cover. Pastor D and Lady T, you are two of the most precious people that I have ever met. Pastor Sharon Dean, thank you for showing up and showing out! Anna, your eyes are beautiful! Pastor Jackie Dixon thanks for the love. Tredd, "Totally Ready" and Justine McDougald, you ran interference at the finish line...... Whew...

Also, I want to give a heartfelt thank you to the countless people who were a sounding board and a tremendous source of encouragement. Thank you for your undying support, for confirming what God has given me, and for urging me to put it in print. I feel that this is a defining moment for the body of Christ! Sherri . "Dancing Queen" Jones, you rock!

Endorsement

First of all, let me start this invitation by saying that this is an awesome woman of God. She is both prophetic and revelatory. I would just like to say that in her poems of excellence she addresses the issues of the heart and the mind. I call them life's essentials, the building blocks to a new life. One, the key to vision is you must have faith. Two, where there is darkness there is no vision. In our many experiences in life these poems are tools to help us deal with life's incidentals.

The first thing I can learn is that if I can change my thinking I can change my traumas into triumphs! I believe what the scripture says "I can do all things through Christ"... (Phil 4:13). Joshua said be strong and courageous. The purpose of these poems is to inspire me and motivate me to new levels of Christ consciousness. It helps me to identify the Christ character that I should see in me (house under construction). I should see more of Christ and less of me. Therefore, my analysis is that this book will help you exceed and excel in life with a clean heart, new thinking and a greater determination to go forward. I can see my future clearly now. I have the tools and the knowledge to accomplish my goals and objectives.

God Bless You,

Dr. Munday Smith, Prophet

Contents

Forward

What can I say about a naturally gifted and anointed individual? Her name is Yvonne Y. Peterson, a rendition of poetry in song. Her lyrical poems flow out of her as rivers of living water. After experiencing her gift, I have a vivid understanding of God's word "He that believeth on me, out of his belly shall flow rivers of living water" (John 7:38). Her poems cuddle and lift your spirit into a realm of new life. Yvonne has finally graced us with printing her gift. And now here it is in your hands!

Enjoy your journey as you move with the flow of this living, anointed river and enter into His peace, enlightenment and profound words of encouragement. When you exit, you will walk into His presence with praise and thanksgiving. As Yvonne always says, "To God be the Glory!"

"Enter into his gates with thanksgiving, and into his courts with praise: be thankful unto him, and bless his name." ~Psalm 100:4

Estela Beckford, M.D.

Introduction

Dr. Mark Chironna's book, *Stepping into Greatness*, **opens up with a statement that is very profound ,"In the pursuit of your life's purpose, there will strategically occur a defining moment in the form of a refining crisis, setting you free from a confining limitation, thus empowering you to step into greatness." [1]Well, thank God for this defining moment. It has finally arrived and God has caused me to tap into some of my treasure.** *Prophetic Poetic Expressions* **emerged at a time when the storms were raging; the rainbow behind the rain is so beautiful. He has given me such an array of anointed poems that should not only encourage but they will set the captives free. It is as though the levee in me has broken and the words cannot be held back. I feel like a pen that He is using to express His love, concern, and intentions to His people.**

What a wonderful time this is basking in His presence and availing myself to be used as a conduit. I know that whatever I am is because of Him and I feel honored that His mind is operating through mine.

---

[1] *Stepping Into Greatness, Dr. Mark Chironna*

Once I chose to enter into His rest, the rivers started to flow to bring renewal and restoration. My prayer is that, Prophetic Poetic Expressions does for you what it is doing for me.

Prophetess Yvonne Y. Peterson

Isn't it great to realize that there is peace in the midst of the storm and there is light in the midst of darkness? As you journey in God, if you do not have the right view, you could think that you are losing ground when you are actually gaining. Once you get the revelation that the way down is the way up, you stop trying to go around the mountain and you speak to it or simply climb it and enjoy the mountain top view.

One

At the Top of the Mountain

At the top of the mountain is where you can meet with God. He is there waiting for you to show Himself to you and express His love for you. He wants to do it in ways that you know not of. There you can have an experience second to none. Your view is broadened and you see panoramically what is happening to you and around you. Mt. Sinai is where Moses met with God. God called him to come up so that He may give him a glimpse of who He is and to also give him instruction since he was a deliverer. God spoke to him from the *"burning bush," (Exodus 3:1-4)*. He was called to a place where most will never go. Moses had an intimate relationship with God. He was God's friend. He spent time learning the ways of God. His job was to ultimately go back to the valley and teach the children of Israel how to have an experience with God as He attempted to lead them out of the wilderness into the promised land, *(Exodus 19:1-25)*.

The mountain top is also synonymous with elevation, a high place. On the contrary, there is the valley, a low place. It is there that we face the intricate, complex things that come along with this life. We are challenged sometimes beyond belief. We have to learn how to stand in the valley, *(Psalm 23:4)*. I propose that the way to do this is to have, "A Mountain Top Experience in the Valley." There are times that you may not want to press in or go on. However, I suggest to you that at those moments God is calling you to come up to the mountain. This can be done experientially, if you know what I mean.

Once you can push pass your flesh and all that comes to distract you, believe me, you can get there. The key is to elevate your thinking. Just think about it, when you are at the top of a mountain and look down, everything that you see at the bottom is so small. That is how you must view the stressors of your life and see that God is bigger.

It takes courage, perseverance, humility and a willingness to come up to the mountain of God. It is for the one who endeavors to have a more intimate relationship, or should I say friendship with God. It is there that you learn how to reverence God. It is also a place where you can see from, as Tommy Tenney puts it, "A God's eye view."

I would also like to point out that Dr. Martin Luther King said that he had been to the mountain top and his eyes had seen the coming of the glory of Lord!! He too was a deliverer. He looked beyond what he was facing and experienced God's glory in an unimaginable way. One might say that he had, "A Mountain Top Experience in the Valley."

After this I looked, and, behold, a door was opened in heaven: and the first voice which I heard was as it were of a trumpet talking with me; which said, Come up hither, and I will shew thee things which must be hereafter. (Revelations 4:1)

A Mountain Top Experience in the Valley

I am having a mountain top experience in the valley
At times it felt like I had been ransacked and left in an
alley
The thing I understand is that I am passing through
While I am here I examine myself too

I cannot lose focus and say that it is not fair
Nor should I become overwhelmed with cares
What I must do while in the valley that is best
I rid myself of an alley mindset

An alley mindset gets you stuck on the bad
You see nothing positive and you are sad
When you put your thoughts on the mountain top
You can tap in to a well that will never stop!

While in the valley do not let it get in you
Think of what you want to accomplish after you make
it through
Glean from this awesome experience
Don't take others or yourself too serious

A mountaintop experience causes me to reverence
The reward is limitless, there is never a severance
I am so glad that I realize my valley is my mountain
Now, I am drinking from a never ending fountain

God Has Revealed, Now Your Blog...

An Encounter of the God Kind

I have so much on my mind
It is about an encounter of the God kind
It is an encounter that takes you on a trip
It is all about communion and divine fellowship

It is all about being madly in love
It is a covenant and partnership with the One above
He helps me daily to renew my mind
I told you that it is an encounter of the God kind

Each day He adds to it and gives me an extension
He stretches me and pulls me into another dimension
His Spirit probes me and brings conviction
What I am experiencing is fact based not fiction

He takes me, holds me, and wraps me up
He tells me to drink out of the God cup
It is thrilling and chilling to partake of this stuff
This spectacular encounter is more than enough

What I like is that it is not just for me
It is for anyone who finds themselves thirsty
Come to this place, it is not hard to find
Enter this amazing encounter of the God kind

God Has Revealed, Now Your Blog...

New Living Water

Did you get some of the new living water?
God is pouring it out on His sons and His daughters
This water knows neither creed nor race
It transcends all time and space

This is coming from a never ending well
It's the outpouring spoken of in the book of Joel
Hurry up, it is not too late
Yield and become a prime candidate

If you would come before Him prostrate
It will flood you at an astronomical rate
It's to prepare you for destiny's date
You will find that it is well worth the wait

You can be last or you can be first
It does not matter; He will quench your thirst
This is beyond anything you could imagine or think
You will never thirst again once you get this drink

Sometimes it gives me the shivers
When I think about these new flowing rivers
They are more than enough from the giver
He is the living water who always delivers

God Has Revealed, Now Your Blog...

Communion is a call to fellowship. It is not just between us and God but it is between us as believers. When we take communion it should cause us to examine ourselves, remember Christ's sacrifice and make sure that we truly love God and our brethren. Our preamble should be, We the people of God In order to form a more perfect "communion" come into divine fellowship to show the world that we are one as we advance the Kingdom of God and prepare for the marriage supper of the Lamb.

Two

Communion - Come on in Union

Come on! Come on! Come on in union! This is what I hear when I think about communion. The Lord has a desire to fellowship with us. At times it is an urgent call, at others it is a pull or tug. No matter how He does it, the reason is to show us how much He cares and desires to let us see His inward parts. This will teach us how to flow with one another on a daily basis.

The ultimate communion, or divine fellowship will be the marriage supper of the Lamb to which we are all invited. I remember, no pun intended, some years ago I wanted a better understanding of communion. I kept asking the Lord to enlighten me and open up the depth of breaking bread and drinking wine in remembrance of Him. Dr. Mark Hanby delivered one of the greatest discourses on the topic that I have ever heard. He called it "The Order of Breaking Bread." He explained that when we have divine fellowship or communion with God that there is no separation or division between us and our mates or brethren.

He further went on to discuss the thief on the cross who asked the Lord to "remember" him when He came into His Kingdom. He spoke of the body of Christ as disjointed and dismembered. Thus, the thief was asking to be remembered or put back together with Him, *(Luke 23:42)*. Furthermore, when we take communion as a body, couple, or family, we should examine ourselves and allow the Lord to remember or join us back together with Him. The Word tells us that many are sick among us because we do not discern His body properly.

Therefore, our will must constantly be broken in order for us to stay in union with the Lord and to come in union with each other, *(Mark 14:22)*. Our earthly marriages should be a reflection of the divine marriage that will take place. The body, the bride is being prepared for her groom who is waiting to spend eternity with her. Come on! Come on! Come on in union!

The cup of blessing which we bless, is it not the communion of the blood of Christ? The bread which we break, is it not the communion of the body of Christ? For we being many are one bread and one body: for we are all partakers of that one bread. (1ˢᵗ Corinthians 10:16-17)

Communion

I am working on cultivating this union
The lover of my soul and I are in sweet communion
He has set aside a place especially for me
He has defined me as royalty

I want you to listen to this
Communion is just sweet fellowship
It starts with a simple invitation
You get invited to spend time with Him in
communication

He tells you how He loves you so
His blessings upon you He does bestow
You tell Him that it is Him you want to know
It is a continued fellowship with a divine flow

Communing with Him is easier than you think
You eat of His body and of His blood you drink
I will never trade this sweet fellowship
I will commune with Him daily and stay at the top of
His list

God Has Revealed, Now Your Blog...

Intimacy

What happens when I go into the garden?
That's between us, I beg your pardon
I will give you a slight peep in
You can see a little of what is up with me and Him

There is not much that I will let you see
That is why it is called intimacy
A special touch, a love filled eye, and privacy
All of these things are associated with intimacy

When I am there He washes away my sin
I repent before Him then I can begin again
He gives me a taste of His delicacies
This is something else that is shared during intimacy

The time spent there, I want it to last
Sometimes hour and hours and hours do pass
When I sit at His feet it's like taking a class
Wow, these intimate times are a blast!

He loves me like none that I have ever known
These intimate moments are ours alone
I will make sure that my heart does not harden
I will stay naked before Him and intimate in the
garden

God Has Revealed, Now Your Blog...

Keep the Fire Burning

The fire is burning
Stir up the coals that fuel your yearning
There are things going on around and about
The enemy wants to distract you and put your fire out

You stir up the fire by staying in the Word
God will give you revelation that you have never heard
When you get off the path and leave the fold
The fire grows dim and your heart turns cold

There is a solution, just start again
Come back to the fold and draw nigh to Him
When you return He will stir up your desire
He will take the torch and relight your fire

God's Word can keep the flames nice and hot
He knows how to torch you in the right spot
Always make sure that your heart is discerning
Fan the flames and keep the fire burning

God Has Revealed, Now Your Blog...

There is an art to communicating a message non-verbally. We are called to be living epistles to be read. What story are you writing when the pages of your life are opened? Endeavor to walk your talk. It is not always easy but we must work so that our words and actions correspond, then others will see our good works and glorify our Father which is in heaven.

Three

Talking Loud Without Saying Anything

I want my non-verbal communication to speak so loud that others will want to imitate me as I do Christ. It would be great to replicate the experience of Smith Wigglesworth who walked in such an anointing that men were brought to salvation without him uttering a word. This makes me think of what the Bible says about us being living epistles to be read of all men, *(2nd Cor. 3:2)*. Wow, if we could collectively shine our light so bright that men could see Him in us, we would be so much closer to the coming of our Lord and savior, (*Matt. 5:16*).

"Action speaks louder than words" is so apropos for this notion. Too many times as Christians our corresponding actions do not line up with our words. This causes us to be ineffective and we are scorned by those who we want to win to Christ. From now on our motto should be, "I can show you better than I can tell you." Then, we should align our actions with our words to say that we are walking our talk. The lines from a secular song say, "Talking Loud and Saying Nothing."

I am working on emulating the Lord by saying nothing unless He says it and doing nothing unless He does it.

When I am able to do this it will speak volumes to a lost and dying generation. Let us be more mindful when we are in the presence of unbelievers.

Let our example be one that they will say, "I did not know that they were Christians but they act like it." We are the only Jesus that some will ever see. It is time for us to pump up the volume!

For thus saith the Lord GOD, the Holy One of Israel; In returning and rest shall ye be saved; in quietness and in confidence shall be your strength... (Isaiah 30:15)

Talking Loud Without Saying Anything

Knowing when to be quiet requires special skill
When you may want to chatter you just stay still
Sometimes to others it makes no sense
But you know that it is all about quietness and
confidence

There is more than one way to say what you need to
say
Taking Loud without saying anything is certainly a
way
Solomon said that there's a time to speak and a time
to refrain
People want to know what is in your brain

Quietness speaks volumes so many times
It makes others wonder what is on your mind
You take the mysteries that have been spoken and you
keep them to yourself
When and if you are released you take them off the
shelf

I have heard the Lord speak and He told me,
"sshhhhhh"
That means don't open your mouth unless I say that
you could
There is something that I am learning about this walk
and everything
You can be talking loud without saying anything

God Has Revealed, Now Your Blog...

The Tongue

There is so much that we can do with our tongue
We can build things up or by it be hung
This tongue can be used to bless
It can also create a disastrous mess

Even though it is very small
It can actually cause or prevent a nation's fall
This member of our body is little in size
It can put others down or cause them to rise

Sometimes we just do not think before we speak
We open up our mouths without being discreet
At other times we can be very constructive
Yet, in the same breath we become very destructive

The Bible says the tongue should be tamed
You see how unruly it can be, isn't that a shame
You simply need to know the truth
Some tongues are actually just too loose

If you meditate on the words from your mouth
You might consider what you allow to come out
You want to be pleasing in God's sight
When you think before you speak, you may get it right

Now you know that we can take a poll
We would find out that most tongues are out of control
Man cannot control it, but I know who can
Just ask God to cover your mouth with His hand

God Has Revealed, Now Your Blog...

Quietness

There is something that people don't think about
when they diet
Part of their regimen should be coming to the quiet
In the quietness you can really think
It makes me want to put my pen to the ink

Quiet time causes me to sit and wonder
During this time I refrain from big blunders
I make sure that I am retrospective
I take time to put things in their proper perspective

In the time of quietness it's not others that I see
I look inward and examine me
I see what it is that I can tweak
When God finishes with me I will be chic

Quietness is described as having no sound
It is when things unravel and become unwound
I further attribute it to being smooth
The effects of it can actually soothe

Heaven knows some of us will never be quiet
We think too much will pass right by us
If you want to see if you pass the acid test
Ask God, "How am I doing with my quietness?"

God Has Revealed, Now Your Blog...

Comprehending the power of prayer will cause us to stay in an attitude of praise and watch the wondrous power of almighty God as He answers us at the appointed time. Prayer releases God's best for us on a regular basis via protection and other innumerable things. Make sure that you pray or continue to pray without ceasing.

Four

Praying Produces Answers

Prayer is so very vast and profound. Yet, it is so simple. It is direct communication between you and God. Thank God for Jesus that we no longer need to go through a priest. He is the High priest and the only mediator between God and man, (*1st Tim. 2:5*). We can go boldly to the throne of grace, (*Heb.4:16*). It is by prayer that this world is framed. It can be one word or an intricate travail. When you go to God either way He hears and answers. I have heard people say that the only thing left to do is pray as if it is a last resort. My response to this is, "What we can do is pray." The answer to everything is as I said, so simple. We pray as if God is not on the throne. However, the Bible says, "For he that comes to God must believe that He is, and that He is a rewarder of them that diligently seek Him," (*Hebrews 11:6).*

Most of us do not enter into serious prayer because it requires discipline. We think it takes too much time. Then there are those of us who simply do not believe in the prayer that we pray, or that God really does answer. We also think that praying requires us to be in a certain position. One thing that we must know is that we must spend time in prayer. The Bible says to pray without ceasing, (*1st Thess. 5:17*).

I have heard it said "little prayer, little power, much prayer, much power."

So, let's think about it. There are times that you may lay prostrate before the Lord for an extended period. You may bow down on your knees as well. Then, there are the times when you have to attend to your daily living whether it is a job, family, or all else. I believe the application of praying without ceasing fits here. You can be in an attitude of prayer that does not require a particular position. When you take on this mindset, no matter where you are, you apply prayer to anything or anyone that needs it.

Dr. Mark Hanby opened my mind to the concept of the doors of prayer. As I have spent time in prayer, I have allowed the Holy Spirit to lead me to and through the right door. It could be the door of intercession, worship, praise or just praying in the Spirit. These are some of the doors that he taught on. Whatever the door, allow yourself to be led and never become religious, or you will be limited in prayer. Never think of it as the last option. Remember, that God is looking for someone to show how strong He is as they stand in the gap, *(Ezekiel 22:30)*!

Whether you are in the car, at the store, in the shower, or in your secret chamber, pray effectually, fervently, incessantly, and expect results.

Confess your faults one to another, and pray one for another, that ye may be healed. The effectual fervent prayer of a righteous man availeth much. (James 5:16)

Therefore I say unto you, what things soever ye desire, when ye pray, believe that ye receive them, and ye shall have them. And when ye stand praying, forgive, if ye have ought against any: that your Father also which is in heaven may forgive you your trespasses. (Matthew 11: 24-25)

Likewise the Spirit also helpeth our infirmities: for we know not what we should pray for as we ought: but the Spirit itself maketh intercession for us with groanings which cannot be uttered. And he that searcheth the hearts knoweth what is the mind of the Spirit, because he maketh intercession for the saints according to the will of God. (Romans 8: 26-27)

Build an Altar

One thing that ensures that you won't falter
You must always build an altar
When you build it in the right place
The scent from it will come up into God's face

Never let yourself get bewildered
Determine to be an altar builder
Building an altar is meant to be fun
You are building it to the Holy One

After a whole lot of wear and tear
Build up an altar of prayer
It has its own recompense
Let your prayers go up as incense

When you build it you must yield
It becomes your protective shield
The altar is established on prayer
God ears are inclined when you are there

You are saying that you don't have space
This kind of altar can be built any place
There is a safe place that you can start
Sacrifice and build an altar in your heart

God Has Revealed, Now Your Blog...

Intercession

What will be our next lesson?
It is all about the art of intercession
One thing that causes you to intercede
Your heart is pricked when you see a need

It is the heart of God that you want to tap
He uses you to stand in the gap
Intercession can be very grueling
It is with the spiritual world that you are dueling

Intercession is a skilled art
All God wants is for you to do your part
Give up even the slightest facade
Let yourself become an instrument of God

Intercession can cause you to become disheveled
That is because you are interfering with the devil
You have to make him loose his hold
A true intercessor is very bold.

You know when you enter the enemy's territory
You are there to set the captives free
Intercessors do not want to be seen
You yield yourself to God, and keep your heart clean

God Has Revealed, Now Your Blog...

Just Pray

Just pray when you think there is trouble
God answers all prayers on the double
You think that the manifestation has been delayed
The answer was given the moment you prayed

You interceded and said "with my prayer I fought"
The Scripture says God's thoughts are higher than our
thoughts
You prayed and hoped that things would be fine
God wants you to know that everything takes time

Prayer is what causes the world to go around
Prayer lifts you up when you are down
Prayer has its own distinct scent
It always hits the target where it has been sent

You opened your mouth and God heard
Prayer is just simply sending the Word
Whenever there is a specific need
Join in with the Lord and begin to intercede

Prayer is something we sometimes don't understand
Prayer was a part of the Master's plan
Though Satan desires to sift you as wheat
Nothing will happen when Jesus intercedes

Whenever you decide to cast your cares
You will find out that the proof is in the prayer
There could be so much more to say
My last comment to you is, "Just Pray"

God Has Revealed, Now Your Blog...

There is a place away from all of the hassles of this life. It is a place where you can be encapsulated by His presence and abide under His shadow. You will be protected and sheltered. It is the secret place..........the safest place that I know.

Five

It is well Because I Dwell

The secret place is where I long to hang out! I could just stay there indefinitely. Well, you can but you can't; it appears to be a paradox doesn't it. What I mean by this is we are seated with Him in heavenly places right? That is by experience; thus, as a result of this we should daily remain in the secret place of the Most High God.

He has taught me to say "It is well because I dwell." I learned a very powerful lesson one day. I was communing with Him on a steady basis. I kept the intimacy going no matter where I was (at home, work etc...). Not only was I enjoying it but God was too. I was interrupted by a couple of co-workers. I left work a little displeased by how I was handled. On the way home I made a decision to walk in love and forgiveness towards them for I was sure they did not fully understand who they were dealing with. I spoke to the Lord and expressed that I did not like how I was being treated but I would respond the way that I previously stated.

When I reached home as I stood in my kitchen the Lord gave me this revelation. He let me know that anytime someone comes against me while I am in communion with Him they have trespassed. Since I abide under His wing, they are interfering with our fellowship. The response that I had was the one that He wanted. He longed to resume our fellowship so He would take care of those who trespassed. He showed me how He would lift His protective wing and remove them. This gave me such a peace that I forgot about the distraction of the day.

When I returned to work the next day I found that God had dealt with the culprits who came to me in an apologetic manner. That experience taught me how important it is not to allow anyone or anything to keep me from staying in the secret place. So, in essence, "It is well because I dwell."

He that dwelleth in the secret place of the Most High shall abide under the shadow of the Almighty.

I will say of the LORD, He is my refuge and my fortress: my God; in him will I trust.

Surely he shall deliver thee from the snare of the fowler, and from the noisome pestilence He shall cover thee with his feathers, and under his wings shalt thou trust: his truth shall be thy shield and buckler. (Psalm 91:1-4)

The Secret Place

I am learning more about God's grace
It causes me to come into the secret place
I have moved beyond visiting
This special place has been reserved just for me

It is where I love to dwell
I do not mind being under God's spell
The spell that I am under is more than just nice
If I stay here forever that will suffice

I am protected by His wings
Just think about it; this is a powerful thing
This is something for me to savor
I love being caught up with my Savior

I do not have to figure out any angles
He has me surrounded by His angels
There is something that cannot be erased
I have authority to camp out in the secret place

God Has Revealed, Now Your Blog...

The Secret Garden

The secret Garden of Gethsemane
That is where He sweat drops of blood for me
It's the place where He agonized
God would not have it otherwise

I wonder about the things that He thought
What great strength to fight the way they He fought
I am so glad that His heart did not harden
The disciples did not stay awake in the secret garden

The secret garden is where He prayed with power
They could not even tarry with Him for an hour
He knew from the father He would be separated
He shows us what it means to be dedicated

In that garden the weight of the world was on His
shoulder
He wanted to please the Father and He became bolder
He submitted His will to that of the father
Had that been some of us, we would not have
bothered

The secret garden is where you find relief
There you cannot be troubled by the thief
It is the place to get a release
It is the only place where you find real peace

God Has Revealed, Now Your Blog...

Angels Watching Over Me

Angels are watching over me
They do their job so diligently
They are on special assignment
The job they have been given is heaven sent

I know that they are all around
They have lifted me up when I almost fell down
When I travel I really feel free
They are on assignment watching over me

I am glad that I understand what they are for
Gabriel is a messenger and Michael is all about war
When I lay down upon my bed
They stay on post and hover over my head

As I enter into a very deep sleep
Some bring messages to me that the Lord tells them to
speak
I am glad that I have insight and that I can see
I must thank the Lord for His angels watching over me

God Has Revealed, Now Your Blog...

When our mind is clear we are free to be creative and open to endless possibilities and opportunities. Healthy thoughts allow us to grow and develop into what the Lord is calling us to be. The mind is where false imaginations must be captured and brought into alignment with Christ centered thoughts. Since we know that the mind is the battleground, we must equip ourselves with the necessary armor to guard it and fight the good fight of faith.

Six

What is on My Mind?

The mind is incredible...It houses our deepest thoughts both good and bad. It can be used to propel us to go in a positive or negative direction. It can keep us up or down. We are influenced by God, Satan, or our own humanness. It is up to us to work daily to think healthy. Our mind is the battleground where there is a war going on. False imaginations must be cast down so that the whole godly thoughts can be enthroned, (*2ⁿᵈ Cor. 10:4-5*). That is why we must do as the Bible admonishes us to do. How we think impacts our emotions. Sometimes, as we think so it is. Some are paralyzed because of past traumatic experiences that cause continuous post-traumatic stress. It is up to us to allow our minds to be renewed on a daily basis. Though it may be difficult it can be done. The Bible tells us that we can be transformed by the renewing of our minds, *(Romans 12:2)*. If the trauma that you experienced has caused you to become stagnant, you may need to have your mind renewed by getting some professional guidance coupled with the Word. The Bible also lets us know that perfect peace can be obtained by keeping our mind on Him, *(Isaiah 26:3)*.

Additionally, Paul urges us to let the mind that is in Christ Jesus dwell in us, *(Phil. 2:3)*. With that mind, we can move past the horrid experiences and everyday challenges and distractions that want to stunt our growth and cause us to miss our date with destiny. If you have been in this position and desire to let go of major or minor hurts and pains, check your thought pattern and make the necessary adjustments so that you might be able to live your life to the fullest. You might say, "I can't." Well, if you truly love the Lord and believe His Word, believe this, "I can do all things through Christ which strengtheneth me," *(Phil. 4:13)*.

As you meditate in the Word it can erase the blemishes of the past, give you a new outlook, and you can also begin to believe who God says that you are so that you can become what He says that you will be. Here is a thought for you, "My mind is playing tricks on me." That is exactly what the enemy wants you to do; he wants you to use your own mind to play tricks on yourself. Then, you will never become who you were destined to be. Yet, there is good news. The Bible tells you that whatever is pure and lovely is what you should be thinking about. If you do this, God promises that the peace which passes all understanding shall be yours, *(Phil. 4:6-9)*. Let me remind you that this must be done on a daily basis in order for you to be successful.

Your Mind is The Battlefield

Your mind is the battlefield
The enemy wants to stop you and keep you still
He wants to keep you in confusion and under duress
The aim is to halt your Godly success

He works on your mind day after day
He uses false imaginations to stand in your way
He tells you that God won't supply all of your need
He gets you to think that you are nothing and that you
can't succeed

He sends you in circles around and around
He tries to take your smile away and place a
permanent frown
He wants you to think you have no reason to live
He tries to convince you that you have nothing to give

He works on you to develop a negative thought
process
He wants you to ruin your own happiness
After a while you become his little toy
Then you tell yourself "I will never have joy"

You start to shed so many tears
That cycle repeats year after year
The Holy Spirit comes to you time after time
He tells you to take authority and quiet your mind

God Has Revealed, Now Your Blog...

_____
_____
_____
_____
_____
_____
_____
_____
_____
_____
_____
_____
_____
_____
_____
_____
_____
_____
_____
_____
_____
_____
_____
_____
_____
_____
_____
_____
_____
_____

Fear

Fear can control you, immobilize and paralyze you
Fear can make you not know what to do
Fear can make you not know what to say
Fear can make you ruin your entire day

Fear can make you quiet or it can make you shout
Fear can cause shame or it can make you doubt
Fear can take you down roads you don't want to go
Fear can cause you to wander to and fro

Fear can make you stay up all night
Fear can have you full of fright
Fear can make you think that you are sick
Fear can play all kinds of tricks

Fear can cause you to stay behind
Fear can make you lose track of time
Fear can pump you full of anxiety
Fear can keep you from your destiny

Fear can make you panic; fear can make you fret
Fear can make you think of danger when there is no threat
Fear makes you worry about what has not happened yet
Fear can make you miss what you are supposed to get

Fear is a spirit sent from Satan to you
Fear wants to keep you from being made new
Satan made it by popular design
It is to stop you from operating in God's Spirit of love,
power, and a sound mind

God Has Revealed, Now Your Blog...

My Shattered World View

God is shattering my world view
He is destroying it to give me something new
It is all about the way that I think
When my thoughts line up, He will give me a drink

There is a reason that He has to shatter
Some of the thoughts I think really do not matter
I must line mine up with His
He wants me to understand the way that it is

If my thoughts are not converted
They will be distorted and possibly perverted
Once I think like Him my thoughts start meshing
After that there comes a great refreshing

If I do not conform I will be left behind
The reality is I must change my mind
If God can change my mind, He can change my season
I must renew my thinking for this very reason

I am open and my thoughts are new
God has completely changed my entire world view
This shattering has greatly impacted my life
The view I now have is from the mind of Christ

God Has Revealed, Now Your Blog...

_____

_____

_____

_____

_____

_____

_____

_____

_____

_____

_____

_____

_____

_____

_____

_____

_____

_____

_____

_____

_____

_____

_____

_____

_____

_____

_____

_____

_____

_____

_____

_____

The wilderness can be an exciting, ambiguous, and sometimes painful place. There you are challenged to solely and wholly follow the direction of the Lord. At times it seems that you might not make it to your destination. However, as you surrender and abandon your plan for His, you will enter the Promised Land!

Seven

Walking through the Wilderness

The wilderness or should I say wild in the nest.....That's how it feels! It is like wild things continue to happen while so much is already happening to you. When God allows you to be led into and through the wilderness, there is no telling what you might go through or when you are coming out! It is a journey that is actually a lifelong process with continual beginnings and endings.

Sometimes you may think that you will not make it or you do not want to make it; but one thing is for sure, if you let God take you through the process you will emerge, like Moses, a mighty deliverer who knows the ways of God with total faith and trust in Him, *(Psalm 103:7)*.

Any great man or woman of God who is called to lead people to the Promised Land.....the place of destiny.....will go through tremendous trials and tribulations. You will wonder many times if God loves you when He allows you to go through or takes you through so much. Rest assured the experience is to get out of you what is not needed and to put in you what you will need.

You will be broken, molded, shaped and reshaped. You will come out victoriously and ready to do Kingdom business. Not only that, you will discover many treasures. It could almost be said that you are on a treasure hunt because during that time you will not only rid yourself of what is not good, you will find all the good there that will define you and cause wealth to come it your hands. That is, when you yield and believe the report of the Lord.

We often hear how an eleven day journey turned into a forty-year nightmare, (*Duet. 1:2*). The length of the journey was extended far beyond what need be because the children of Israel murmured, complained, and did not follow the instruction of the Lord. While this is true and they should have gotten there sooner, the wilderness is a place that is necessary for the process of refinement. God allows us to go there so that we can be prepared, leave the worst of us there and, bring the best of us out. When you are led into the wilderness, like Jesus, *(Matt 4:1)* when you come out the enemy will not be able to find anything in you, (*John 14:30*). Moreover, you will have a broader view and understand that the wilderness is about process and preparation, not punishment.

Isolation

Isolation is for insulation
God shields you from devastation
During isolation you may feel lonely
But it is a time for you and God only

You may not even get a call on the phone
Isolation makes you think that you are all alone
There is one who really has something to say
It is God so He moves others out of the way

Isolation is a time of incubation
God nurtures while you are in preparation
Don't get troubled during this isolation period
God is doing something that will make others curious

During isolation you are being sequestered
You are separated from some things that pester
It can be a time of great pain
What follows could amount to great gain

It is a time to solidify your relationship
It is certainly not a time for you to trip
It is a time for you to develop
You must recognize that you are being enveloped

Isolation is not a time of punishment
It is more about advancement
Here is what I think is the most
It is about getting closer to God as well as your growth

God Has Revealed, Now Your Blog...

The Wilderness

When you are in the wilderness
You must not walk through in distress
Your labor is not in vain
Cease to murmur and complain

You are just being formed
The wilderness creates the perfect storm
Do not camp out and start to cry
Remember, in the storm safety is in the eye

If you fail to grasp the lesson of this phase
For you it will be a never ending maze
God desires to bring you out
Instead of a stance of victory, you continue to pout

Because you refuse to see what is wrong
This Promise Land is being prolonged
The wilderness is a place designed to prepare
An eleven day journey turned into a forty year
nightmare

Determine to become more discerning
Walking through the wilderness is intended for your
learning
It is time for you to really get wise
Act like Joshua and Caleb when they went in like spies

When they expanded their vision look what they saw
They were unlike the others with their evil report

They refused to fear the giants and they took a stand
While the others perished they advanced to the
Promised Land

You must know that God is taking you someplace
Get to know His ways as He shows you His face
When like Paul you learn how to abase
You will walk through the wilderness with elegance
and grace

God Has Revealed, Now Your Blog...

Wilderness Medicine

There is a weight that I must jettison
I do it while taking wilderness medicine
It is essential for the next leg of the journey
I must let it be taken out on a gurney

Wilderness medicine encompasses laughter
It guides me through times of disaster
Wilderness medicine is about maturity
It solidifies that God is my security

The wilderness causes me to search for God's Love
I relish all that He gives from above
Wilderness medicine causes me to dance
I realize that nothing happens by chance

Wilderness medicine causes me to forgive
It unlocks treasures that cause me to live
Wilderness medicine gives revelation
It makes me further cherish my salvation

Wilderness medicine causes me to shift
It breaks all barriers and gives me a lift
Once I except what happens in that place
I shed my pride and look into His face

God Has Revealed, Now Your Blog...

Transition implies that you are in between and on your way somewhere. Caterpillars are in transition and are making their way to becoming butterflies. Transition can be both smooth and uncomfortable. We play a major part in the outcome of our transition. As long as we allow ourselves to be led, God will cause the end result of our transition to exceed our expectation.

Eight

Times of Transition

Transition means that you are in between. It is as much a part of life as the air that you breathe. It can be a place of uncertainty. Also, it may be a lonely, frightening experience; but as long as you understand that it is temporary, there can be quite a lot gained by being there. There are times in our lives when we are going from one place to another. During this time we should take inventory and examine why we are there. If we assess the experience appropriately, we will emerge with wisdom. Additionally, we could actually obtain what is needed to cause us to excel even though we may appear to be having a setback. You are not left alone; the Lord is with you to bring you into something new, *(Isaiah 43: 18-19)*.

This period can prove to be fruitful if we allow it to. Transitional periods can involve so much. They may entail the loss of so many different things as well as a change in your spiritual, physical, mental, emotional or social situation. These are just some to name a few. Whatever the transition may be just know that it will not last forever. These time periods do not always have to be tumultuous. I am sure you have heard of "A smooth transition." How we handle transition throughout life will determine if we are the better for it. I have had an array of them in the previously mentioned areas and I have grown and benefitted from them all. However you choose to look at or face yours is entirely up to you. You may use it as a stepping stone or you can allow it to immobilize you and block the very blessings that have been designed for you.

I would like to think of mine as an opportunity to move from a lesser truth to a greater truth as well as know that I am looking through a glass darkly. I may not know what is on the other side of the situation but I believe that I am being moved closer to God and what He intends for me.

For now we see through a glass, darkly; but then face to face: now I know in part; but then shall I know even as also I am known. (1st Corinthians 13:12)

Journey

I keep thinking about the journey
The end of this portion is for what I am yearning
There is something that I am discerning
I cannot go forward without learning

This journey seems to take so long
I keep walking and singing a song
My mind just keeps on turning
The fire within me won't stop burning

I think of the journey and my making
I stop focusing on how long it is taking
I examine my heart and extend my hand
Jeremiah twenty-nine eleven says that God knows the
plan

What a magnificent place concerning this station
The journey is more than a simple destination
There is much to explore, glean, gain and venture
This journey, it has become an awesome adventure

God Has Revealed, Now Your Blog...

I Am Working on You

I am working on you, I am working on you
Stop trying to tell me what to do
You act like I am in your hands
You think that you are the one with the master plan

You're trying to tell me about the perfect time
I Am Kairos, I am the Divine!
Stop telling me about your biological clock
Keep your eyes on Me and just watch.

I hold the key to everything
It's not for you to worry about a thing
When you realize who holds the key
You will say "It's you Lord, no, it's not me"

I am taking you on a journey
It will bring you into your destiny
You don't know what is on My mind
Just rest assured that you will be on time

God Has Revealed, Now Your Blog...

Transformation

Despite the torrential rains of this storm
A transformation has been going on
You wonder about so much devastation
I can only say it is part of the process of
transformation

You think what is happening is without reason or
rhyme
Let me inform you that transformation takes time
Just when you thought that everything was through
You found that God was not finished with you

You need to know that everything will be fine
You are being transformed by the renewing of your
mind
You can remove all doubts and fears
The transformation has taken place over the years

You are called to bring unity
You are anointed to beautify the community
You have been given all of the information
Now you must transmit it and induce transformation

You say that you don't know what you did
Transformation took place while you hid
You had some questions and you asked why
You have changed from a caterpillar into a butterfly

God Has Revealed, Now Your Blog...

_____
_____
_____
_____
_____
_____
_____
_____
_____
_____
_____
_____
_____
_____
_____
_____
_____
_____
_____
_____
_____
_____
_____
_____
_____
_____
_____
_____
_____

Entering the rest of God is what we should be striving for. God has so much in store for us, but we must learn to take Him at His Word and enter in. That place of rest is a promise and it could stop us from being overly concerned about so many things. Remember, God rested and He is our example of how to cease from our labor.

Nine

Enter In

It takes time to enter God's rest. The Bible says that we must labor to do so. I am sure that you recognize that the word labor implies that there is work involved. Now, exactly how much work, it depends on you! What I mean by this is that how we interpret and internalize life and our perception of God will show whether or not our hope and trust is in Him. As we become more intimate with God, entering into His rest should become easier. Time, experience, and maturity are all catalysts for achieving this. There is a rest that is promised to the people of God. Our faith must be coupled with the Word of God. Additionally, we must cease from our own labor in order to enter in. This is where the real work or labor comes in. It means allowing God to be totally in charge knowing that He has our best interest at heart.

God did not tell us to enter into stress! He encouraged us to enter into His rest. As I spoke of labor, I discussed it as hard work. Well, for some women it is easy and for others it is laborious. There are those who barely labor and deliver easy births. On the other hand, there are women who spend hours in labor and end up having a painful cesarean birth or do not deliver at all. That has set my wheels to turning.

Many of us choose to take God at His Word and trust Him making our journey through the complexities of life less painful or laborious. Joshua and Caleb are two great examples. Yet, there are the rest of us who emulate the children of Israel and we labor and miscarry, have premature, still born, or deformed visions and dreams. Thus, we forfeit entering into the Promised Land. Either way, there is work involved. Please, do not let your labor be in vain. Some of us have such a difficult time with the thought of releasing everything to God because we are not used to it. However, I have come to understand and accept that this is the prerequisite for entering His rest. Once you make a decision to do this, you will be able to accomplish much more than you have ever imagined. You will let God bring you to a place of surrender and you will begin to receive His best, spirit, soul, and body.

¹Let we therefore fear, lest, a promise being left us of entering into his rest, any of you should seem to come short of it.

²For unto us was the gospel preached, as well as unto them: but the word preached did not profit them, not being mixed with faith in them that heard it.

³For we which have believed do enter into rest, as he said, as I have sworn in my wrath, if they shall enter into my rest: although the works were finished from the foundation of the world.

⁴For he spake in a certain place of the seventh day on this wise, And God did rest the seventh day from all his works.

⁵And in this place again, if they shall enter into my rest. (Hebrews 4: 1-5)

Enter God's Rest

We must start to enter God's rest
Do it in spite of all of the trials and tests
Now is the time for us to learn
Our heavenly Father is most concerned

He has not abandoned you
Just persevere until you see your breakthrough
Entering God's rest is easier than we think
If we keep our mind stayed on Him we would be in
perfect peace

When you enter the rest of God
You will receive the very best from God
God knows all about your trouble
As you enter His rest, He will give you double

This is such an important time
God's rest will take a load off of your mind
It's time for you to embrace the Divine
Enter God's rest and all else will be fine

God Has Revealed, Now Your Blog...

_____

_____

_____

_____

_____

_____

_____

_____

_____

_____

_____

_____

_____

_____

_____

_____

_____

_____

_____

_____

_____

_____

_____

_____

_____

_____

_____

_____

_____

_____

_____

_____

Anxiety

I started thinking about anxiety
It is one of the pressures of life and this society
I thought about what would happen if I took a poll
Most people would tell you that they are in control

The trouble with this very thing
The one who should be in control is the King of Kings
Anxiety can get all in the way
It makes you forget to supplicate and pray

You tell yourself that you are not going to worry
Then your thoughts shift back to anxiety in a hurry
If you could only get it through your head
You would accept that there is nothing to dread

The reason that you are having so many scares
You forget to be anxious for nothing and to cast your
cares
If you get in the Word, meditate, and listen to me
You would lift your eyes to the hills and stay anxiety
free

God Has Revealed, Now Your Blog...

Daily Bread

I never have to worry about being fed
God always supplies my daily bread
Daily bread is about my need
God has more than enough to feed

He takes the time to hear my cry
He feeds me out of His abundant supply
I do not even have to try
He just wants me to continue to soar and fly

He has told me that the lilies do not toil
You never see the rest of His creation in turmoil
All you must do is wrap yourself in His love
He is El Shaddai the one that is more than enough

You should not worry about tomorrow, next week or
next year
Concentrate on today because that's what is here
Set your affections on things above
Sufficient today is the evil thereof

Never spend time trying to obtain wealth
Focus on God, others and not just yourself
If you could just get it through your head
God will take care of you; He is your daily bread

God Has Revealed, Now Your Blog...

It is so easy to lock into this world system and forget that we are making a pilgrimage. Despite the constant onslaught of what may seem like unbearable trials and tribulations, we are passing through on our way to eternity where we will be relieved of the stressors and pressures of this life. Let us learn not to hold on so tight and truly begin to wear this world like a loose garment.

Ten

Wearing the World like a Loose Garment

I was thinking of what it means to wear this world like a loose garment. This is a very complex thought to me. We never seem to consider what the garment may be; thus, we have to wonder whether or not we will disrobe when the moment arrives. We say that we will but when we have to let go of a loved one, a job, a friend, money, or possessions, most of us have a difficult time.

I am learning that we must truly forsake all for Christ. All of the aforementioned, especially loved ones are important, but everything must be kept in its proper perspective in relationship to the Master of the universe. He takes priority over all else. When we do not abandon all to advance in the Kingdom, we can become weighed down by all of the things that impact upon our lives.

I do not want to diminish the fact that this world is a beautiful place and we have been given so much to enjoy. Our family, friends, and all of the precious gifts that have been laid at our feet are very important but they are still temporal. To wear this world like a loose garment means to be in balance. God knows what we feel as the traumas and experiences of life take place. We will have emotional ties to so many things. I am not suggesting nor implying that you should not care about anything. Yet, I am saying that if you believe what the Word of God says in reference to us being pilgrims passing through, over time, you will learn not to hold on too tight.

Things are fitting a little loose for me right now. I hope and pray that when the next challenge presents itself the garment will come off easily.

Dearly beloved, I beseech you as strangers and pilgrims abstain from fleshly lusts, which war against the soul. (1st Peter 2:11)

Loose Garment

There is something that the Word warrants
You must wear this world like a loose garment
Do not hold on to things too strong
When you do, so much goes wrong

We forget that we are just pilgrims passing through
We hold on too tight that's what we do
The real end to our destiny
We will leave here to spend eternity

What I try to think about each day
I am passing through, I am on the way
The painful things that happen here
They won't continue when I get there

The reason that God gave His Son
It was to redeem us and to show the way home
I love this world, but I am not charmed by it
That is why I wear it like a loose garment

God Has Revealed, Now Your Blog...

Excess Baggage

I was taking a plane ride and found that my baggage
was no longer free
The sky cap handed me a receipt and it said excess
baggage fee
This whole concept prompted in me so many thoughts
The more you hold on to needless things, the more
you become distraught

Excess baggage can be so many things and there is a
cost
If you let it there will be nothing left and all will be
lost
You must learn how to travel light
When you jettison dead weight you can take flight

Excess baggage piles up over time
You become full of clutter especially in your mind
All of that baggage is nothing but sin
Repent and do your first works over again

As you rid yourself of the heavy load
God's grace will place you on a different road
Don't let excess baggage get to you
Lay aside the sin and the weight that so easily besets
you

God Has Revealed, Now Your Blog...

The Sacred and Secular

There is something that is spectacular
I am learning how to balance the sacred and the
secular
You must understand your calling
Once you do there will be no falling

I am certainly not suggesting that you compromise
What I am suggesting is be very wise
There is a time to move and a time to be still
What I mean is that it takes a whole lot of skill

Paul said he learned to be all things to all men
We must learn this lesson from Him
If you use the right methods when you go fishing
You will catch men without missing

Whether it's the board room or on the street
You must be selective and discreet
The sacred is like a precious pearl
Remember, you are in but not of the world

God Has Revealed, Now Your Blog...

The fruit of the spirit is all about character development. When our fruit is ripe others want to taste and see that He is good. There should be a daily inspection to determine if our fruit is ripe and that we are bearing fruit that will remain.

Eleven

Can I Inspect Your Fruit?

When I think of the fruit of the spirit, I think of how much I fall short. I can take a yard stick and surely see that I do not measure up, (You are supposed to laugh). Anyhow, what I am saying is that I could use a whole lot more because I have been found lacking. I may be very patient but if I examine some of the other eight fruit of the spirit; I fall short.

I realize that cultivating the fruit is a daily task that I must work on. God knows that it is so easy for me to say that I am not there yet; but so much time has passed in some areas I should have been there and back, (that called for more laughter and a Selah). I guess what I am really trying to say is, if you have been walking with Christ any length of time, you must begin to examine your fruit and you should also be bearing some.

The Bible says that you will know them by their fruit. In this day and age we are always challenged. Where I may be patient...I may not always have self-control. As previously stated, it is a daily and difficult task to balance and demonstrate the right fruit consistently. However, as we determine to yield to the Holy Spirit who leads and guides us into all truth, we will begin to show that our fruit is ripe and ready for picking and tasting. There are all kinds of fruit. If someone examined your fruit what would they find? Would it be putrid, not ripe, over ripe or just ripe enough?

On the other hand, some of us have no fruit. The Word tells us that God prunes us to bear fruit. If we have no fruit, as we allow the pruning process we will begin to bear some. Then, for those of us who are at the thirty fold phase the pruning process will cause us to be moved to the sixty fold phase and for those who are at the sixty fold phase we will be moved to the hundred fold phase.

I am not trying to make anyone feel bad, but I am challenging you to desire what is good so that you will yield a more peaceable fruit of righteousness; also, you want others to know you by your fruit.

Ye shall know them by their fruits. Do men gather grapes of thorns, or figs of thistles? Matthew 7:17

Every branch in Me that does not bear fruit, He takes away; and every branch that bears fruit, He prunes it so that it may bear more fruit. John 15:2

But the fruit of the Spirit is love, joy, peace, longsuffering, gentleness, goodness, faith, Meekness, temperance: against such there is no law. (Galatians 5:23)

What's up with Your Fruit?

You say that you are walking in truth
I want to know what's up with your fruit
You try to be so unassuming
Just know that God is going to do some pruning

When someone comes near me I am a detector
I have become a proficient fruit inspector
I don't' care how much they pretend
You can tell that there is no fruit in them

Sometimes there is no gentleness
Most times you see there's no love
It's as if you think that you won't be found out
But you are being watched by the Master above

One thing that I can say with assurance
You show that you know nothing about endurance
Let me ask this for instance
Don't you know that you are supposed to exhibit
temperance?

You continue to fail the patience test
If you allow me, I will tell you about the rest
You have forgotten something important my friend
The fruit of the spirit, there are nine of them

God Has Revealed, Now Your Blog...

Pruning

God is doing some fine tuning
He is taking you through the process of pruning
Do you understand what this will do
It will cause you to bear more fruit

Pruning can be a painful process
It is designed to facilitate fruitfulness
Do not even think about your age
You can bear fruit at any stage

Pruning must be done on a regular basis
It is necessary to bear fruit in the right places
When God prunes He will not harm you
It is certainly not meant to alarm you

You say "I want it done all at once"
But that is not how pruning is done
Just as it is with fine wine
Pruning takes place over a period of time

Why are you being pruned this way?
It is to multiply the fruit that you bear each day
When all is said and done you will see
You will remain a fruit bearing tree

God Has Revealed, Now Your Blog...

The True Vine

This is a sentiment of mine
I am so glad that I am connected to the true vine
Anything else is nothing but a fake
As long as I stay connected I minimize mistakes

I have to explain this to you next
If you are overburdened there must be a disconnect
The true vine signifies you are in Him and He is in you
No matter what happens He will see you through

There is nothing to worry about when you are in
trouble
Call on Him and He will be there on the double
Your connection gives you special rights
You are given authority to win the fight

He is the truth, the light and the way
I marvel at this divine connection each day
At times it is painful and at others I pine
I will never trade anything for the true vine

He is the one who always delivers
He is also more precious than gold or silver
He prunes me and makes me very astute
I am connected to the vine to bear much fruit

God Has Revealed, Now Your Blog...

Wow.....walking in the spirit...if we could only grasp the understanding that we really are spiritual beings having a natural experience...

While on this journey we fumble and stumble in pursuit of our destiny. There are times that we may be focused and determined to walk in the spirit and demonstrate or reflect the character of Christ. Yet, we are sometimes challenged beyond belief to balance our daily Christian walk.

Twelve

Walk On!

Too many times we are not living up to our Christian values. We say that we are made in His image but we sure do not act like Him. We also say that we want to be like Him, but we are far from measuring up to that standard. The world is looking at us and does not like what it sees. More than that, we should not like what we see.

No, we are not perfect, but we should be striving for perfection. We use the excuse that Christ is the only perfect one. Well, in some sense that is true; however, let's examine that a little closer. Christ came to show us that we too can step up to the task. Remember, He took on the form of man so that He would be challenged and tempted, yet be without sin, (**Heb. 4:15**). Thus, you can too, because it was not the divine Christ who did this; it was the man Christ.

When we speak of perfection, it is actually maturity that is being spoken about. The Greek word used here is "teleios." "Teleios" means mature or complete. What I am actually saying is that I use this paper as a mirror to bring myself in line. I must hold myself accountable through the Word and make a decision to be mature and walk in the Spirit. We have to learn how to naturally walk in the spirit. There will be a lot of trial and error involved, but it is a lifestyle that can be attained. As you become more conscious of the fact that the supernatural should be second nature, you will avail yourself to the Spirit of God, and allow Him to show you how to develop your supernatural walk. I love the lyrics to a song that say, "You are not a natural being having a spiritual experience, but you're a spiritual being having a natural experience."

This walk requires us to understand discernment and be in tune with and very aware of our surroundings. Otherwise, we will not walk in the spirit and we will fulfill the lust of the flesh. Walking in the spirit makes one cognizant of the fruit of the spirit and you opt to utilize them when dealing with and responding to the carnal or natural man. Furthermore, it could simply be life's situations that frustrate you to no end and you forget that you live in the spirit. When you are spiritual, you exhibit the fruit of love as opposed to hate and you work on being slow to anger, which requires the fruit of long suffering. Actually, when you master the fruit of love it overpowers the entire negative or evil that is thrown your way and it neutralizes the powers of darkness that attempt to keep you in the flesh.

Yes, you will fall short at times, as it may take years for you to walk so circumspect that you are able to say, "...It is no longer I that liveth, but Christ that liveth in me...." *(Galatians 2:20)*. You must practice this on a daily basis, actually, moment by moment. Let me give you a good example. The Williams sisters did not start out being avid tennis pros. It took them years of practice to develop and become world renowned champions. So it is with walking in the Spirit. The Williams sisters had to deny their flesh to accomplish their goal. They had to sacrifice. The real challenge is that most people around us tend to walk in carnality and go for what they know. The Holy Spirit has the responsibility to lead and guide you into all truth. So, rely totally on Him to get you there. As you yield moment by moment, day by day, and year by year, you will eventually become a spiritual pro. As long as you understand this, you will be able to respond in the spirit when you are challenged or confronted by that which is in the flesh. My admonishment to you is, walk on!

If we live in the Spirit let us also walk in the Spirit. (Galatians 5:25)

Walking in the Spirit

There is something to walking in the Spirit
It requires doing the Word when you hear it
You must also have great concentration
You prioritize and give much dedication

No one hinders you from obeying the truth
You are not bound by the law and you want to show
the fruit
A spiritual walk keeps you circumspect
You love God so much that you give him the utmost
respect

As you walk in the spirit from the law you are free
There is no entanglement with bondage, you walk in
liberty
Exuding from you is an heir of maturity
You stay cleansed and show forth purity

You come to the altar at the simplest behest
You make sure that the fruit opposite does not
manifest
You work to give God your very best
Most of all, you rid yourself of the works of the flesh

You may not get it all at once
But that does not mean that it cannot be done
When you find that the fruit is absent
Yield to the Spirit as you repent

God Has Revealed, Now Your Blog...

Dead Woman/Man Walking

I love God and it is Him that I am stalking
In order to do this I must be a dead woman/man
walking
It is me that He decided to employ
The job is my flesh, crush, kill, and destroy

When I am bombarded with thoughts in my head
I am not impulsive; how can I be when I am dead?
Dying to self is a moment to moment process
It is the only way to have real success

I know that it is an ongoing process
This death also eliminates a whole lot of stress
The reason that I must crush, kill and destroy
I am not about to allow anyone to steal my joy

There is nothing that you have to dread
Detach yourself from carnality so that you stay ahead
There are so many things that can cause you to balk
They can actually hinder your spiritual walk

I see the enemy and his ploys
But I have a spiritual walk that I must enjoy
I just have to get it through my head
I had a funeral for my carnality, and now I am dead

God Has Revealed, Now Your Blog...

_____
_____
_____
_____
_____
_____
_____
_____
_____
_____
_____
_____
_____
_____
_____
_____
_____
_____
_____
_____
_____
_____
_____
_____
_____
_____
_____
_____
_____
_____
_____

Spirit, Soul, and Body

Something great is happening to me
God is working spirit, soul, and body
I will try to explain as much as I can
He is working on the total man

All of this must be in harmony
This is the only way that we are free
It is also how we can be healthy
The total man that will be me

The spirit and the soul are at war
Yield to the spirit and the soul won't score
You have been given power over sin
As your spirit, soul, and body line up, the total man
begins

The total man can be intricate
You must know how to work all of it
So what am I doing in my life?
I am disconnecting from all things that create internal
strife

I may not be able to do it all at one time
Yet, I am getting control of this life of mine
When all is said and done, I will be rid of calamity
I am entering a new realm spirit, soul, and body

God Has Revealed, Now Your Blog...

Finding contentment is a daily struggle. With all of the things that bombard us day to day, even moment to moment, we can fluctuate in our emotions. Yet, when you have an encounter with the true and living God, you begin to understand that no matter what state that you are in, contentment is not dictated by circumstances.

Thirteen

Content with Content

For years I wanted to be in a place of contentment and I have finally arrived. Like Apostle Paul, I do not count myself to have apprehended, but I believe that I am there. It took some time but I have acquired something that qualifies me to be in this place. What is it? It is developed faith? That faith simply shows that no matter what is going on; God has and will continue to see me through.

Furthermore, let's think about it, Paul was more qualified to say that he was content in whatever state that he found himself. Paul was beaten, shipwrecked, bitten by a snake, and thrown into jail for the sake of the gospel amongst other things. Yet, he could say, pen, and live those words. Contentment denotes satisfaction; thus, he was saying that no matter what was going on, whether he had, or did not have, he was content. One ponders the thought of how could Paul be satisfied after facing the aforementioned atrocities. I would think that it had to be directly related to his faith. That means that Paul had strong, great or developed faith. Paul experienced something to get him there. It is quite obvious he had to get a revelation of who God is in order for his faith to be so strong thereby arriving at a place of satisfaction.

Well, let us think about ourselves, or I will use myself for an example. What happens when I am not content? Part of it may have to do with the situation or circumstance that I find myself in. The discontentment that I experience is because I do not want to go through anything that might resemble pain. If I focus on what I am going through, I cannot move on. What must happen is I, like Paul, must get the revelation of who God is to me. When I am focused on my present state, I am showing that I have little faith or underdeveloped faith. However, once I determine to accept that God is bigger than the present circumstances; I can advance, become content, and that revelation causes my faith to be developed. When I do this repeatedly my faith should continue to develop. So, I too arrive at a place of satisfaction or contentment.

Let's discuss more of how I think that Paul was able to be content. Remember, content means to be satisfied. Then there is content; same spelling, different word, pronunciation, and meaning. Look at the definition, *something that is contained: the contents of a box; the subjects or topics covered in a book or document*. Ah! My wheels are turning again. Do you think, like I do, that contained within Paul was content, meaning the volume of the book, meaning, Jehovah Jireh, Jehovah Shalom, and all else that He is? Not only do I think it, I truly believe that Paul was content because he had content. Therefore, his joy, peace, and financial situation were not predicated upon his present circumstances. Paul had righteousness, peace, and joy in the Holy Ghost. You and I would do good to recognize this and apply it so that we too can be satisfied no matter what. Not only will we be satisfied, but we will drink from the cup of contentment.

8Finally, brethren, whatsoever things are true, whatsoever things are honest, whatsoever things are just, whatsoever things are pure, whatsoever things are lovely, whatsoever things are of good report; if there be any virtue, and if there be any praise, think on these things.

9Those things, which ye have both learned, and received, and heard, and seen in me, do: and the God of peace shall be with you.

10But I rejoiced in the Lord greatly that, now at the last your care of me hath flourished again; wherein ye were also careful, but ye lacked opportunity.

11Not that I speak in respect of want: for I have learned, in whatsoever state I am, therewith to be content.

12I know both how to be abased, and I know how to abound: everywhere and in all things I am instructed both to be full and to be hungry, both to abound and to suffer need.
(Philippians 4:8-12)

Content

I did not know that it would go the way that it went
Like Paul, I had to find a way to be content
I placed myself in a position to wait
I learned how to operate in whatever state

The cares of this world would flood my mind
I kept thinking that I was losing time
I realized that God's way was not my way
He showed that things were not denied even though
they were delayed

Content means that you are satisfied
When you walk with the Lord this area will be tried
When it seems that your life has come to a halt
Place no blame on yourself; it is not your fault

When God is ready there will be success
Know that He has given you the key, and is willing to
bless
Stay before Him and daily repent
As you master these principles, you will find yourself
content

God Has Revealed, Now Your Blog...

Be Still and Know

Be still and know that He is God
For those who tend to be anxious that's a big Job
Don't you know His promises He keeps
He always takes good care of His sheep

Be still and know is a must
It only requires mustard seed faith and trust
There are times that you do not trust the father
You may act like Peter and teeter-totter

The truth about be still and know
It is leaning on God and letting go
It is gaining your inheritance while being meek
With blessed assurance you rest at His feet

It causes you to walk in quietness and confidence
In your weakness He increases His strength
It is all about not being in a hurry
You rely totally on Him and abstain from worry

There is constant communion between you and Him
The stillness comes when you enter in
Once you grasp the reality of be still and know
You stay in sync and continue to flow

God Has Revealed, Now Your Blog...

The Lines Have Fallen to Me in Pleasant Places

The lines have fallen to me in pleasant places
They are filling up the empty spaces
I keep listening to hear what is said
I get it onto the spaces and out of my head

He is my portion, He fills my cup
I want more of Him so I keep lining up
With patience I continue to run this race
I rest in the fact that He will keep me safe

He is my inheritance and my lot
I accept what He says is and what is not
He will never let you be disgraced
He will cause all of the lines to fall into place

There is something about the lines falling into place
You must know that you can't do it at your own pace
In order to keep the lines falling into place
I must fall in line and seek His face

God Has Revealed, Now Your Blog...

There comes a time after you have been faithful spiritually and naturally, you want to know when you will be given the opportunity for advancement. Ultimately you, like Joseph, will be remembered by God and at the appointed time promotion will come.

Fourteen

Promotion

Most of us think that promotion comes after hard work or passing a test. In many instances this is true. However, there are too many times when we do all of the above and it appears that nothing seems to happen. Well, I want to inform you that there is no need to be discouraged. The truth about the matter is that promotion comes from the Lord. He is the one who puts one down and sets another up. The problem is that most of us do not understand this.

Whatever you deserve will come to you eventually. Let it be within God's time frame because that will be the best and right time. Our motives must always be right in order for God to promote us. Oh, we know that some put themselves in position and say that God did it. Also, they never bring honor to His name or allow His light to shine while they are there.

Just know that when one is elevated by the Lord, it is for His purpose although He will allow you to reap many of the benefits that are associated. Never think that your day will not come no matter how long it may seem to take. Your time is at hand; you have persevered and shall get the promotion that you deserve.

God has a twofold promotion in store for many in the spiritual and natural arena. If we could only fathom this, more time would be spent promoting the Kingdom as opposed to being overly concerned about promoting ourselves. Continue to rejoice and wait in earnest expectation for what the Lord is about to do for you. Joseph is a classic example of one who stood the test of time and was elevated beyond his imagination, (**Genesis 41:39-41**). It was in three phases---from the pit, to the prison, and finally to the palace.

I said unto the fools, Deal not foolishly: and to the wicked, Lift not up the horn:

Lift not up your horn on high: speak not with a stiff neck.

For promotion cometh neither from the east, nor from the west, nor from the south.

But God is the judge: he putteth down one, and setteth up another. (Psalm 75:4-7)

Promotion

Promotion comes after passing a test
It does not come from the south, east, or the west
The Word promises this very thing
It comes from the north, the city of our great King

People do things that are a shame
They try to bring attention to their own name
They make this terrible mistake
When you lift Him up, He will make your name great

What should be the root of your promotion?
The impetus should be your Godly devotion
It has been since time began
God has always elevated a man

The plan was for His purpose
Too many never delve beneath the surface
It is hard for some to relate to it
When you are about His business there are side
benefits

So many people have missed it.
They act like the promotion is all for their benefit
There is something that is extra nice
You get promoted by God while leading others to
Christ

God Has Revealed, Now Your Blog...

Certified

You have been through the fire and thought you had
been fried
God has stamped His approval and deemed you
certified
When you started out your life was a mess
You had to go through the rigor of many great tests

God certifies you for His own use
When you allow the full process you will be Satan
proof
He takes you and uses His glove
He touches your heart to see if it's full of love

After some time has passed and you show endurance
He will let you know that there is blessed assurance
You had sleepless nights and many you may have cried
It wasn't for naught; you are now certified

At the end of the road after you have counted the cost
He will restore the years that you thought were lost
Now, He can use you and there will be no removal
Even though others don't; you have His approval

God Has Revealed, Now Your Blog...

Your Gift Will Make Room for You

Your gift will make room for you
It does not matter what people do
They can talk about you and tell their lies
They can try to mask their hate as love in disguise

When God unveils you, there will be no doubt about it
There is absolutely nothing anyone can do about it
The gift that He gives is not just for you
It's to show others Jesus and give Him, His due

The gift can open many doors
If you use it for His glory, there is much more in store
You should allow God to use you at His own pace
He will give you the wisdom to endure this race

Your gift will cause you to be empowered
The blessings will come and you may be showered
Pride can go before you and cause you to stumble
Let your gift make room for you and you will remain
humble

God Has Revealed, Now Your Blog...

There are times of silence in everyone's life. At times it seems unbearable, especially when it seems like God does not hear you. You wonder will your time ever come and will you emerge from the place of testing and trials. You do not want the vision that is placed on the inside of you to die. Well, just think about Jesus and His years of silence. In between twelve and thirty, He too was tested greatly during His silent years. Once the volume was turned up there has not been silence since.

Fifteen

The Silent Years Speak

There is a place and time in your life that you may feel like God may not be listening or you are not hearing. You may feel and think that heaven is like brass. You know that God's hand is upon you and that you are supposed to be going somewhere. Sometimes, you may have an inkling of the direction that you are headed in; and at times you need and want more clarity. What many of us do not understand at that time is, we are in a place of development. This is an incubation period that will cause you to develop properly so that you can kiss destiny head on.

This time can evoke a great degree of frustration and restlessness. You may think that you are forgotten and forsaken. What you must realize is that God is with you and has your best interest at heart. He knows what it will take for you to go the distance and represent Him to the best of your ability. He has to place you in protective custody from yourself and others. These are the years when the baby that has been birthed must be taken care of so that it will become viable and thrive!! When a baby is born you do not let just anybody handle the baby. You also may not just let anyone see the baby right away. There are also times that the baby is so beautiful that you don't want to say much or brag on the baby. This might cause people to become envious or jealous and they may even try to harm the baby.

The silent years are a time to read the Word, pray, travail, worship, praise, and truly wait on the Lord. Do as they say," Whatever you may find your hands to do." Take care of the baby and know that the end result will be beyond your wildest imagination. Speaking of imagination, you must cast down all types of imaginations that would try to make you think that you will remain in an unfilled state, (*2ⁿᵈ Cor. 10:4-5*). You are actually waiting on the fullness of time. That is why it is important for you to do all of the above things that have been mentioned. When you do them consistently, eventually the fullness of time arrives and you emerge. You will be ready for what the Lord has promised. You begin to get more direction and clarity. You start to connect the dots and realize that it has been precept upon precept; line upon line, here a little, there a little, (*Isaiah 28:10*). Suddenly, what seemed like the silent years begin to speak voluminously. Not only do you hear them speak, so does everyone else within ear shot!!

And thine ears shall hear a word behind thee, saying, This is the way, walk ye in it, when ye turn to the right hand, and when ye turn to the left. (Isaiah 30:21)

The Silent Years

These have been the silent years
They have been full of many tears
God had to allay all of your fears
Things were not what they appeared

It may seem like God was silent
What was going on is that He was the pilot
You were preoccupied wondering about your station
Yet, He was taking you to your destination

At times it seemed like you were in class
Other times it appeared that heaven was like brass
You knew that you had made the right choice
All you wanted was to hear His voice

It took a long time, but it is finally here
He gave you no more than you could bear
There were some things that He was tweaking
Now, the silent years are loudly speaking

They have a lot of things to say
Like how God guided you through day by day
How He anointed you and filled your cup
Thanks are to God how He has turned the volume up

God Has Revealed, Now Your Blog...

I'm Coming Out

I'm coming out and I won't doubt it
I'm in full bloom and the petals have sprouted
I'm coming out, that's what I hear
God is telling me to remove all fear

I'm coming out, I have passed the test
I have left Egypt behind and all of my mess
I'm coming out, I have made it
God has confirmed that I have graduated

I have broken out of my shell
I still continue to say," It is well"
God has shown me nothing is a waste
He continues to help me to walk by faith

I'm coming out, I have celebrated
This is the moment for which I have waited
I'm coming out, I'm taking a stand
I have entered into the Promised Land!

God Has Revealed, Now Your Blog...

Your Time to Shine

This is your time to shine
God will make sure that you do just fine
It is not about your plight
He wants to use you as His beacon of light

He will put you on display for others to see
His glory shall beam giving you the victory
Sometimes you will look like a beautiful bouquet of
roses
Then at other times you will have the radiance of
Moses

You have shown that your light is so bright
You dispel the darkness of the night
You seem to attract people wherever you go
Your countenance always gives off a special glow

Let His light continue to come through
He has chosen to shine forth in you
He has you in the forefront of His mind
Just know that this is your time to shine!

God Has Revealed, Now Your Blog...

The Writer's Charge!

This is the hour for you to write
There is nothing to fear everything will be alright
The thoughts are there they want to flow
Just pick up your pen it's time to go

You say you don't know if you can
You forgot that God's hand is over your hand
You act as if you have writer's block
The time has come and you must not stop

God has placed so much in you
The release is here it's time for your breakthrough
It's not about what you think
If you would just take the charge, the Spirit will supply
the ink

To contact the author, Yvonne Peterson, email focusedfaithyp@gmail.com

P.O Box 8237

Glen Ridge, NJ 07042

www.ingramcontent.com/pod-product-compliance
Lightning Source LLC
Chambersburg PA
CBHW051842090426
42736CB00011B/1924